Copyright ©2021 THEO WILLIAMS MD

All rights reserved. No part of this publication may be reproduced, distributed, or transmitted in any form or by any means, including photocopying, recording, or other electronic or mechanical methods, without the prior written permission of the publisher, except in the case of brief quotations embodied in critical reviews and certain other noncommercial uses permitted by copyright law.

Contents

Introduction 4

Distilling 5

How Distilling Works 8

Basics of Home distillation 12

    Fermentation 12

    Distillation 13

    Filtration 13

    Achieving the desired alcohol strength 14

    What's your flavour ? 14

Getting started 15

    Essential Oils And Hydrosols 17

    Fermentation. 21

    Measuring the strength of your alcohol. 24

    Filtering your alcohol. 24

Step-by-Step Home Distilling 25

    Operating a Pot Still 27

    Foreshots 31

    Heads 32

- Hearts 32
- Tails 32
- Aging 33
- Redistilling 33
- Boiling Temperatures of Alcohols 34
  - What's important to understand before they get started? 36
  - What spirits are the easiest to produce at home? 37
  - What are some good places for hobbyists to source equipment and ingredients from? 38
  - What does a good home still set-up typically look like? 38
  - What's the legal status of home distilling? 39
  - Any distilling tips you're willing to divulge? 40
  - How do you age when you're home distilling? 41
- How to Make Cornflake Whisky From Start to Finish - Hand Crafted Corn Whisky at Home. 42
- Conclusion 44

Introduction

Before going any further, please be aware, home distilling without proper licenses, permits, bonds, and local authorization is illegal. There is no way around it. Making the decision to distill spirits illegally carries both threat of fines and imprisonment. Doing so, should not be taken lightly.

However, that hasn't stopped many people. People all over the world are buying small, "home-sized" stills and distilling up some of their favorite cloned spirits. If you like Jack, Jim, Crown, or Patron, with a little bit of practice and some determination, you too could distill the same spirits, if not distill something better.

In 1996, New Zealand became that rare thing – a country where home distilling spirits is legal. Since then the ranks of distillers have swelled. It's not just alcohol that's made, but fragrant, home-crafted essential oils and herbal distillates, called hydrosols. Johanna Knox takes a closer look at this beguiling hobby.

At its most basic, distillation involves heating a liquid until it becomes vapour in order to seperate out certain components. It is essentially the same process that occurs in nature when surface water evaporates in the sun, rises into the sky and condenses in the clouds to become rain.

Distilling

Distilling is an art that's been used since ancient times for medicinal and spiritual purposes, to purify water, and to create balms, essences, and perfumes. The distilling process can be a lifesaver when it's used to remove salt and other impurities from water – including heavy metals, poisons, bacteria and viruses. For more indulgent purposes it can be used to make alcohol and home-crafted essential oils.

During distillation, a liquid mixture is boiled in a still and the vapour captured and recondensed. The most volatile components evaporate first, allowing you to separate out all the different ingredients of a liquid mixture. Handily, alcohol and many fragrant botanical substances are highly volatile.

Once home distillers have mastered the basic art of distilling, they can produce artisan items at a fraction of their retail cost, while indulging in a fascinating hobby. Small changes in ingredients, environment and process hugely affect the end result, so the learning process is an ongoing one, and the potential recipes and combinations almost limitless.

In 1996, New Zealand became that rare thing – a country where home distilling spirits is legal. Since then the ranks of distillers have swelled. It's not just alcohol that's made, but fragrant, home-crafted essential oils and herbal distillates, called hydrosols. Johanna Knox takes a closer look at this beguiling hobby.

At its most basic, distillation involves heating a liquid until it becomes vapour in order to seperate out certain components. It is essentially the same process that occurs in nature when surface water evaporates in the sun, rises into the sky and condenses in the clouds to become rain.

During distillation, a liquid mixture is boiled in a still and the vapour captured and recondensed. The most volatile components evaporate first, allowing you to separate out all the different ingredients of a liquid mixture. Handily, alcohol and many fragrant botanical substances are highly volatile.

Once home distillers have mastered the basic art of distilling, they can produce artisan items at a fraction of their retail cost, while indulging in a fascinating hobby. Small changes in ingredients, environment and process hugely affect the end result, so the learning process is an ongoing one, and the potential recipes and combinations almost limitless.

Stills come in a huge range of shapes and sizes – everything from giant industrial contraptions bursting with metal pipes and dials down to little plug-in gadgets that look a bit like a benchtop coffee grinder. One of the simplest distillation devices is the pot still, consisting of a single heated chamber and a vessel to collect purified alcohol. Other types include alembic stills, column stills, reflux stills and solar stills.

But all stills have four key components: the heat source to boil the water, the holding tank which contains the water as well as the plant material to be distilled (this sits just above the water), the condenser to collect and cool the steam, and finally the separator, which divides the essential oil from the water vapour.

How Distilling Works

America's new craft distilleries use high-tech equipment to make their whiskey, gin, and other spirits. But they rely on the same laws of fractional distillation a difference in boiling points that allows them to separate ethanol from water that humans have been using to make booze for centuries.

- Distiller

The distiller mixes yeast, water, and sugar (or a sugar-containing grain) in a fermenter, aka a mash tun. After three to seven days of voracious fermenting, the yeast has consumed most of the sugar, turning the mash into a wash (10 or 12 percent alcohol by volume). A pump moves the wash into the pot of the still.

- The Pot

A boiler pumps steam into a jacket, or two-walled metal sleeve, that surrounds the bottom of the pot. The heat builds for a half-hour or so to raise the wash to its boiling points—plural. Ethanol boils at 173 degrees F; water at 212.

- The Distillation Column

As blended alcohol and water vapor rises from the pot, it enters a cool copper column. Most of the vapor condenses and falls back into the pot as reflux. Flat copper condensing plates can span the column, controlling the pace of the process (and the taste of the product). The vapor with the highest alcohol content, and thus the lowest boiling point, continues to the outlet at the top of the column.

- The Lyne Arm

Concentrated alcohol vapor enters a horizontal pipe called a lyne arm. Precise heat is key. Too hot and the vapor contains excess water; too cool and not enough vapor enters the arm.

- The Condenser

Vapor in the lyne arm flows into a vertical chamber, where a pipe of cool water surrounds a pipe of alcohol vapor. As vapor cools, it condenses into liquid ethanol, which drips from the condenser into a collection vessel.

- The Distillate

The first 5 percent of the run, aka the foreshots or heads, contains large amounts of cogeners, or volatile chemical compounds such as acetone, aldehydes, esters, and fusel oils. Next comes the hearts, the high-proof alcohol base. Distillers mix the hearts with small quantities of heads, and the blend is diluted and aged to make spirits. With too high a percentage of cogeners, the drink tastes rough; with too little, it's bland. The last bit, the tails, is a low-proof mix often set aside and redistilled later.

- Aging Barrels

The clear liquid emerging from the still is called moonshine, white dog, or white lightning. It is colorless and harsh. But after a few years in oak barrels, it takes on color, richness, and complexity of flavor. Bourbon whiskey is aged in new but charred oak barrels. Scotch whisky resides in old bourbon barrels, and Irish whiskey ages in used sherry casks. Gin, ideal for impatient distillers, takes on its character once the white dog is redistilled with a botanical blend stirred into the pot.

Basics of Home distillation

Home distillation of spirits is illegal in many countries including Australia. Therefore unless you are in New Zealand consult with your local legislation before you use the information provided in this section.

Fermentation

Fermentation occurs when sugar is converted to ethanol (alcohol) by yeast. During the process sugar is broken into various compounds. To achieve fermentation you will require turbo yeast, which comes in a wide range to suit different climate and conditions. Some of the turbo yeasts available at Malthouse home brew include Alcotec 48 Turbo Yeast, Alcotec 24 Turbo Yeast and Vodka Star Turbo Yeast (the cleanest of them all).

Distillation

A distillation device called a still is used to separate the alcohol from the water in the fermented mixture. The process involves heating the mixture. Alcohol reaches boiling point before water which means it vaporises first. The still cools down the vapour forming drops of liquid alcohol (distilled spirits), which can be collected outside the still. Our distillation units include the Still Euro 5 All Stainless Reflux and Still Mk5 Pot Stainless Steel Condenser.

Filtration

In this step the distilled spirit is run through a filter to get rid of any unwanted impurities and smells. The filtering is done using a carbon mixture and a filter paper. You can purchase Carbon Reflux 400G, Carbon Contact Reactive 300G, Carbon Filter 400G and Carbon Treatment 500G.

Achieving the desired alcohol strength

The alcohol level of the distilled and filtered spirit could be as high as 95%, which is poisonous. The desired level for spirits is around 40% and 22% for liqueurs. Water can be added to dilute the spirit to the right alcohol level. To measure the level you will need one of our Spirit hydrometers.

What's your flavour?

Your spirit is now ready to be used in creating the drink of your choice. To do this you can choose from our range of spirit and liquer essences. Visit our Spirits and Liqueur product page for a wide range of products including books on home distillation

Getting started

The first thing you need when distilling your own spirits is a 'wash' – a fermented liquid. This could be as simple as a cheap bottle of wine. Run it through your still and watch as, like magic, a smaller quantity of spirit emerges from the condenser, its alcohols and flavours concentrated.

The 'heads' dribble out first, containing the most volatile compounds, including acetone and methanol. You will need to throw these away, unless it's nail-polish remover you're after. Next come the 'hearts', brimming with ethanol – drinking alcohol. Make sure you keep this liquid! Lastly, the 'tails' bring less volatile compounds such as propanol. To ensure you get rid of the heads, one rule of thumb is this: for every 20 litres of wash, throw away 50mls from the start of the run.

Tracking the temperature of your vapour is another way to determine what stage of the run you are at. For example, ethanol vapourises at around 78°C (although this varies slightly with factors such as altitude). Once your vapour reaches that temperature, you know the hearts are emerging.

Even more fun is fermenting your own wash. Make up a sugar-rich liquid using anything from a simple syrup to a mash of fruits, grains or vegetables, plus yeast. You can attract wild yeasts (like making a sourdough starter), but it's more reliable to use a commercial product, such as baker's yeast or one of the many wine-maker's yeasts available for sale online or at specialist stores. These commercial strains are often known by uninspiring names such as CY17 and R56. However, a dealer will be able to tell you exactly what each strain is best used for. Vintners Harvest Yeast SN9 is known as one of the best all-purpose yeasts. It's ideal for beginner efforts, and easy to get hold of in New Zealand.

Adding extra nutrients can help your yeast grow and reproduce. To do its work, yeast needs nitrogen, oxygen and trace amounts of various vitamins and minerals. Specialised nutrient mixes are available from distillation suppliers. However, many home distillers swear by simply adding a little tomato paste to their wash.

Over days, the yeast converts the sugars to alcohol and carbon dioxide. To determine when your wash is ready, you can use a readily available device called a hydrometer to measure its alcohol content, or you can do a simple taste test. Is the wash still very sweet? If so, it means there is plenty of sugar left to be converted.

After running the wash through your still, the resulting spirit can be cut with water to reduce the alcohol content. It can also be aged, that is, left to mellow and absorb new flavours. Try ageing it with oak chips. You might also add flavourings, such as herbs, spices or citrus peel – use your imagination. You can also choose from the many commercial flavourings available.

Essential Oils And Hydrosols

Place fresh herbs or other aromatic plant material in your still and cover them with water. Turn on the heat, monitor the temperature, and collect your fragrant creation at the other end – a minute quantity of essential oil floating on top of a fragrant hydrosol (sometimes called herbal or floral water).

This process is called hydro distillation. Some stills also allow steam distillation, which at times produces a better-smelling product. The plant matter is supported above the water, and the steam picks up the volatile aromatics as it rises.

With smaller home stills and a backyard's worth of plant material, you'll never produce more than a few millilitres of essential oil at a time, even from plants with a high oil yield. However, a lot of hobby distillers are perfectly happy to experiment and enjoy their boutique homemade products.

With a small home still and a backyard's worth of plants you can create your own boutique essential oils

Producing citrus peel oils is especially revelatory. Typically citrus oils have a short shelf life, and many you buy in shops have already lost their zing. The first time you inhale the fragrance of fresh, home-crafted citrus oil it's like discovering the difference between homegrown and supermarket veggies.

Eucalyptus, fresh root ginger, lavender, rosemary and thyme also yield plenty of oil – approximately 5-20mls per kg of plant matter. You'll need a large-ish still to distill this quantity though. That, or put through several runs in a row.

Once seen as a cheap byproduct of essential oil production, the tasty, fragrant, and cosmetic qualities of hydrosols are now appreciated in their own right. They contain diluted, suspended essential oils as well as plant acids – and this acidity means they keep well. For more on hydrosols.

Once you've got the basics mastered, you'll discover lots of inventive uses for your marvellous, multi-purpose hydrosols. You can use herbal distillates as skin toners, fragrant body sprays, linen sprays, and air fresheners. Jill Mulvaney of Alembics New Zealand suggests using them creatively in the kitchen. Here are a few ideas:

- Make refreshing drinks by adding 30mls of hydrosol to 1 litre of water. Try peppermint, rosehip, elderflower, lemon balm and bay (served with lemon slices).

- Try orange hydrosol added to cake icing, jellies or any cold cooking.

- Mist a rosemary hydrosol over a leg of lamb or a similar dish just before serving to stimulate taste buds and prepare your guests for a delicious meal.

- Add robustly flavoured hydrosols to sauces. Possible base herbs include thyme, rosemary, sage, Vietnamese mint and coriander.

- Try adding a dash of black pepper hydrosol to vodka!

Things to do; Sterilise all equipment before use.

Things you will need;
- 30 litre Fermenter fitted with airlock and tap.
- Stick on digital thermometer 10 - 40 degrees C
- Spirit Hydrometer
- Alcometer
- Measuring jug.
- Carbon Filtering Unit.

- Still.

Fermentation.

- Fill sterilised fermenter with 19 litres water at 40 degrees Celsius.
- Add 9 kgs of Dextrose - this will result in a drop of water temperature to 35 degrees Celsius.
- Use stirrer to mix until Dextrose is dissolved
- Sprinkle Alcotec 24 Turbo Yeast on the surface of the Dextrose and water mix and secure lid and fit airlock.
- Stand the fermenter in a place where the air temperature is between 15 and 30 degrees Celsius.
- When the hydrometer reading is stable for 24 hours and the reading is below 990 S.G

Fermentation is finished:
- Use Finings to remove any yeast and other solids before

transferring the mix to the boiler.
- Transferring the mix to the boiler.
- Unseal the fermenter lid to allow air in when tap is opened.
- Collect the first 100 mls from the tap and discard as this first run through the tap may contains lots of solids.
- Run the mix into the boiler. When you get down to the last bit of the mix tilt the fermenter to get the last bit of the mix out, taking care not to disturb the yeast and other solids off the bottom of the fermenter.
- Fit the lid complete with the condenser to the boiler making sure that the spirit outlet is not over either of the elements.
- Insert the glass thermometer that came with the boiler into the black bung. The thermometer should protrude through the bung by 20 mm. Fit this to the top of the Condenser.

Distilling the Mix using the Reflux Still:
- Fit the two cords to the still and plug into a power supply. Both elements are used to heat the unit up but it is necessary to disconnect one during distillation. Turn on the

water flow to the condenser.
- The mix will take about 1 hour to start boiling. Before distillate starts to come out of the condenser, water should be flowing through the condenser at about 1 litre per minute (This could be higher in warm conditions or slower in cold conditions).
- When the mix is boiling and the thermometer reading starts to increase, but before distillate starts to drip out of the condenser, one of the elements should be disconnected.
- Use one element during distillation
- Collect and discard the first 50 ml of distillate.
- Collect a further 3.5 litres. Stop collecting distillate if the thermometer rises above 90 degrees Celsius or if the strength of the distillate falls below 60%A/V.
- Overall the distillate collected should be approx. 80%A/V if it is lower in strength than this then more water should be run through the condenser next time. If it is higher than this then it is likely that you will not have collected 3.5 litres and less water could be run through the condenser next time you run the still.

Measuring the strength of your alcohol.

Float your alcometer in the spirit and read the hydrometer on the line that cuts the surface of the alcohol. The higher the strength of alcohol, the further down the alcometer will float in the liquid.

Filtering your alcohol.

After you have collected your alcohol it then needs to be filtered.

First water your alcohol down to 50%A/V approx. The impurities are more easily removed when the alcohol is lower in strength. If you have collected 3.5 litres at 80%A/V then you will need to add 2.6 litres of clean drinkable water to bring your total to 5.6 litres.

Open the tap fully and collect the spirit that runs through the filter. Recycle the first litre of spirit back to the reservoir and then collect the rest.

Once you have collected all the spirit then check the strength and water down to 37.5%A/V.

An easy way to work out how much water to add is to measure the quantity of spirit collected and check the strength.

Multiply the quantity by the actual strength and divide this by the required strength. This will give you the amount of alcohol you should have. 5.5 litres @ 55% would be calculated as follows. 5.5 x 55 = 302.5 - 302.5 divided by 37.5 = 8 litres.

In this example you will need to add 2.5 litres.

Step-by-Step Home Distilling

Making "eau de vie," or fruit brandy, at home is easy and safe when you use a pot still. Learn the ancient craft of home distilling and connect with a long tradition of hospitality when you offer your homemade "eau de vie" to visitors. To start distilling at home, you'll need some technical knowledge about the equipment, process and how to handle the delicious results.

Start small and cheap. You can produce flavorful eau de vie using a tea kettle and a condenser made with plastic tubing to distill wine made from a few pounds of fruit. If you know you are interested in home distilling and don't need a test still, then the first still to purchase is a 1 1/2- to 2-liter copper alembic pot still. These often ship from Europe and represent a comparatively small investment for what could become a lifelong hobby. The small still is good for small batches of anything, and for redistilling alcohol you have produced in a larger still.

The largest still appropriate for home use is 5 gallons (25 liters), a size that matches the scale of home-scale fermenting buckets. But even one run in a 5-gallon still makes a substantial quantity of alcohol. While it is always nice to dream big, stills holding less than 1 gallon (4 liters) encourage you to be creative and keep the enterprise well within the bounds and spirit of home-scale craft distilling.

Operating a Pot Still

- Heat source: Stills under a few liters are best operated over natural gas or propane, and ideally in a water bath. This is because when distilling for maximum flavor, one needs to keep the distillation as slow as possible. It is easier to control the heat in a small still if it is indirect.

- Getting ready to distill: Clear a work area around the heat source you will use for the distillation. You will need the following:

- the still
- the wine
- a ladle
- a dozen small glasses to collect the distillate
- a pitcher for mixing the alcohol you are saving to drink
- a jar with lid for the saved drinkable distillation
- a jar for "heads and tails" if you plan to redistill them at some point
- a permanent marker that writes on glass

- a mixing bowl along with flour and water to form the paste for sealing joints
- and a damp sponge and towel for use polishing the still and cleaning up spills.
- If your still will need polishing either inside or out, then also have on hand vinegar and salt.

- Preparing the still

Make sure your still is clean. If copper sits unused for a long time it naturally oxidizes. The traditional way to polish the interior of a copper is to warm it slightly and then pour some vinegar (1/8 to 1/4 cup for small still) into the still, chased by a tablespoon of salt. Then spread with a sponge. You can polish the exterior of your still with vinegar and salt as well.

- Place the pot still over the heat source.

If using a water bath, set the still in a pot that is large enough to be 3/4 immersed in water. For example, a 2-liter still comfortably sits in a dutch oven. Next, fill the still approximately 3/4 full with the wine to be distilled and then assemble the still. The wine can foam up when first heated so don't overfill.

- Assemble the still.

This usually means placing the lid on the distillation pot, running the tube from the lid to the condenser coil, adding cold water to the condenser, and finally putting a glass under the spout through which the alcohol will flow. As most home distillers improvise, their setup it may take a little adjusting to get it working.

Once the still is assembled, make sure fittings are tight. For example, on a homemade still, ensure that any corks or rubber stoppers are tightly in place. All loosely fitting joints need to be sealed. In a traditional copper alembic still, this means sealing where the lid fits into the pot and where the copper tube leading from the swan's neck lid fits into the condenser coil. A thick paste made of flour and water is the traditional sealant.

If using a water bath, use aluminum foil to make an improvised lid around the still if practical. This reduces energy use and reduces evaporation from the water bath.

If the condenser coil is not already surrounded by cold water, add the cold water now.

Operating the Still: The simple part is operating the still. There are just two rules: go slow, keeping the alcohol coming out of the still at no faster than a drip a second, and use lots of jars or glasses to collect the distillation so that after your run, when your judgment is better, you can throw away what is bad and keep the good.

- Turn on heat under the still.

Start with a strong flame and if you are distilling in a bain marie, bring the water bath to a full boil. Once you become familiar with your still, you will get a sense of when the alcohol will begin flowing. From time to time, touch the copper tube close to the lid and also close to the condenser. The alcohol will begin flowing soon after the copper becomes hot where it enters the cooling water. I often notice steam beginning to rise from where the copper enters the water just before or just as alcohol beings to flow. It is especially important not to allow the still to get too hot. The ideal speed is no greater than 1 drip a second.

Your nose is what you use to separate the "run" into its component parts: the foreshots, the heads, the heart, and the tails. The heads and the tails may be saved to redistill. The hearts are consumed, though depending on taste, they may be diluted with water first. There isn't a clear separation between the different parts of the run. The art and craft of distilling is how the distiller makes the call using his or her nose.

Foreshots

The first alcohol to come out is called the foreshots. The foreshots are heavily contaminated with acetone and methyl alcohol. The still does not create these alcohols, but it concentrates them. In quantity, acetone and methyl (wood) alcohol are poisonous. They also smell horrible. Learn this smell. You cannot go too slowly at this stage. The foreshots are thrown away.

Heads

The heads contain a mix of the undesirable alcohols and an increasing percentage of ethyl acetate, which is one of the important flavor compounds in grape wine, and methanol. Most commercial distillers save the heads to run through the still a second and third time. You may want to save them, toss them, or add at least some to the hearts. There is no fixed rule.

Hearts

The hearts is the main run of ethanol. The smell is bright and fresh and is strongly evocative of the underlying fruit or herb in fruit wines and fruit and herbal macerations. As you maintain the still at a steady slow drip you will find that you are slowly increasing the temperature of the still. One drop every second, or even every two or three seconds is what you are looking for from a small still. Collect in small glasses, like shot glasses.

Tails

At some point the flavor changes, becoming more dilute (more water vapor is condensing) and the smell is less pleasant. At that point you are sliding into the tails. The tails contain a high percentage of water mixed with ethanol and fusel alcohols.

Aging

If you smell any of the undesirable alcohols of the foreshots and heads, you can leave the alcohol in a glass container with a cheese cloth lid. After a few days the acetone and methyl alcohol remaining will evaporate. Changes do take place within the glass. Letting the alcohol rest for a few months mellows the drink and reduces any metallic tastes picked up from the still.

Redistilling

Commercial distillers focus flavor by running the alcohol through the still two and three times. Each time through the still a more refined cut of foreshots, heads, and tales is made producing an ever cleaner hearts. The trouble with redistilling on a home scale is that one has to start with an awful lot of alcohol to get enough to run back through a still, and then heating a pot filled with now highly flammable alcohol as opposed to heating wine in a first distillation clearly poses safety issues. It isn't something I'd do in my kitchen nor is it something I'd do over or near an open flame. My advice is to be methodically slow about your primary distillation, gather the run in lots of small containers so you can make the cleanest, brightest mix possible, and be happy with what you have achieved.

Boiling Temperatures of Alcohols

The following is a list of the temperatures at which the different alcohols boil at sea level. In the real world liquids evaporate at temperatures below their boiling point. For example, water evaporates out of ice and snow and rain evaporates off of sidewalks even on cool days under cloud cover. Therefore, there are no clear demarcation points. As the acetone boils out of the wine at 134 degrees, ethanol and water are evaporating too, even though they are below their boiling temperatures. But the steam rising from the still at 134 to 147 degrees is richer in acetone and methanol than in ethanol, so these are the foreshots.

A pot of boiling waters boils for a long time before all the water evaporates. Thus, it isn't as if your wine reaches the boil. What you can see from this table, though, is that to isolate the acetone and methanol, you want to go very slowly so the temperature of the wine creeps up to the 172 degrees of the ethanol, the alcohol that is at the heart of the run. If you go slowly, then it will be clear where the foreshots and heads separate. Everything above ethanol (boldface) listed below is the foreshots and heads; ethanol is the desirable middles; and everything below the Ethanol is the tails.

- Acetone: 134 degrees Fahrenheit (56.5 degrees Celsius)
- Methanol (wood alcohol): 147 degrees F (64 degrees C)
- Ethyl acetate: 171 degrees F (77.1 degrees C)
- Ethanol: 172 degrees F (78 degrees C)

- 2-Propanol (rubbing alcohol): 180 degrees F (82 degrees C)
- 1-Propanol: 207 degrees F (97 degrees C)
- Water: 212 degrees F (100 degrees C)
- Butanol: 241 degrees F (116 degrees C)
- Amyl alcohol: 280 degrees F (137.8 degrees C)
- Furfural: 322 degrees F (161 degrees C)

What's important to understand before they get started?

The first and most important thing to understand is that it's illegal. Assuming you're okay with breaking the law, you can move on to the next bit. You'll need a still, which is generally an expensive piece of equipment, though it can be built inexpensively. A good sized (eight-gallon) hobby still will run you $300 or more. The still is essentially a heat source to boil the fermented liquid to steam (alcohol has a lower boiling point than water) and a cold water loop to create cold surface area inside the still for the steam to condense and collect.

Beyond that, you'll also need everything that you would need for home brewing beer or wine, so stockpots, carboys, big plastic tubs — nothing unusual, but the big sizes can be hard to track down. All the grain, yeast and other ingredients can usually be found in a home-brew shop or grocery store.

What spirits are the easiest to produce at home?

For distilling, I recommend starting with something that's already fermented (I used a jug of Carlo Rossi red wine) and then distilling that to get the hang of using the still before going through the process of fermenting. You don't want to spend a week creating the perfect fermentation only to mess up the distillation at the end. So starting with store-bought beer or wine is a good way to get the hang of the still.

Once you move into fermenting your own mash or wash, most people like to start with sugar (basically a fermented simple syrup). You can add grains for flavor, but the sugar-wash moonshine is hard to mess up. Grains are more finicky, but rewarding. Anyone who has made beer has a leg up in this regard, so if you're comfortable with home brewing, home distilling from grain to make whiskey will be easy. Wine to brandy is basically the same process, but from fruit instead of grain.

What are some good places for hobbyists to source equipment and ingredients from?

Let's say you want to make a homemade bourbon. You can find cornmeal easily enough, but you'll probably want to get ground rye and ground malted barley from a homebrew shop. Most homebrew shops carry a variety of yeasts, and one that's designed for distillers will give you better flavor and yield than a baker's yeast (which will work) or a brewer's yeast (which can be finicky). Good sites for hobby stills are brewhaus.com, hillbillystills.com, or milehidistilling.com.

What does a good home still set-up typically look like?

Assuming you have a stock pot for mashing and a big plastic bucket for fermentation, the last step in the process is the still. Stills come in all kinds of configurations, but the simplest and most traditional is the best: a pot still, basically a closed pot with a tube running out the top, along with some kind of heat source. Because explosions are common around stills, an electric hot plate is safest. The tube from the top of the pot needs to run through a bath of cold water, so many stills have a copper coil that runs through a bucket of cold water. Once you turn on the hot plate and wait for the still to boil, the steam will travel through the tube and into the cold coil. There it will condense and run out the end of the tube. Once you collect this, you have a very crude distilled spirit.

I would recommend taking off what comes out of the still in a single distillation and run it through the still a second time. After the second time, the middle part of run is usually the best anything that's coming off the still in the 65-80% range is usually drinkable.

What's the legal status of home distilling?

It's illegal to run a fermented beverage through a still to produce spirits; hell, it's even illegal just to own a still for alcohol production. So while you can make beer and wine for your own consumption, distilled spirits are still a federal crime. That said, the federal government does not prosecute distillers, but works with local and state police. Some states are more friendly to hobby distilling than others. Best advice is to produce limited volumes, keep a low profile on social media, and be especially careful in NC, FL, AL and VA, where there are frequent moonshine busts.

Another thing is that the federal government requires the manufacturers to supply the TTB (formerly the ATF) with the names and addresses of people who have purchased stills. You're allowed to apply for a fuel ethanol permit, which allows you to make ethanol (whiskey is ethanol, but so is 10% of most gasoline). That's usually a good thing to have just in case you have to explain your still.

Any distilling tips you're willing to divulge?

Not everything that comes out of the still is delicious. The middle part, the "heart" is usually the best. The first part, the "heads," can be solvent-y and taste like nail polish and the later part, the "tails," can be funky and skunky like bad beer. The heads and tails can be collected and aged for future distillations. So finding when to collect the whiskey and what to recycle back or throw away can be tricky. I suggest collecting the distillate in small mason jars and then rather than obsessing over the cuts during the distillation, you can simply choose which jars you like after the distillation is done and that can become your "heart."

How do you age when you're home distilling?

Aging at a small scale can be tricky. There are oak chips that do a good, but imperfect job of mimicking what happens inside a barrel. You can also get miniature barrels that hold 2-5L of spirit. These can be notoriously leaky and can overage if you aren't careful. That said, white whiskey is often underrated, and people are often surprised that moonshine can actually stand on its own if made well.

How to Make Cornflake Whisky From Start to Finish - Hand Crafted Corn Whisky at Home.

Ingredients:

- 5 Liters hot water
- 12 liters cool water
- 4kg Refined white sugar
- 700g Cornflakes
- 20g Still Spirits Whisky Yeast
- Juice of one lemon

Instructions:

- Start by machining the cornflakes until fine in your food processor.

- Pour the sugar into a 25 liter fermentation drum and ad 5 liters of hot water.

- Put the cap on the drum and give this a vigorous shake until all of the sugar has dissolved.

- Pour in the lemon juice, followed by the ground conflakes.

- Add another 12 liters of cool water to the drum.

- Pour in the Still Spirits Whiskey yeast and allow this to stand for 15 minutes before stirring this in gently.

- This yeast contains amyloglucosidase enzymes which convert the complex sugars in the corn to simpler structures resulting in a better fermentation and a broader spectrum of aromatics and flavors.

- Leave the drum open overnight.

- The following day, screw on a cap with a fermentation lock.

- Allow the mash to ferment for 10 to 14 days. At this stage, the bubbling will have stopped completely and if you taste a sample, the mash will have no sugar left at all as this has been converted to alcohol.

Conclusion

Distilling is an art that's been used since ancient times for medicinal and spiritual purposes, to purify water, and to create balms, essences, and perfumes. The distilling process can be a lifesaver when it's used to remove salt and other impurities from water – including heavy metals, poisons, bacteria and viruses. For more indulgent purposes it can be used to make alcohol and home-crafted essential oils.

CPSIA information can be obtained
at www.ICGtesting.com
Printed in the USA
LVHW051103170723
752673LV00007B/443